# SEASONS OF A
# BROKEN HEART

## GIANNA MONTAGNO

*Seasons of a Broken Heart*
Copyright © 2025 by Gianna Montagno.

**MILTON & HUGO L.L.C.**
4407 Park Ave., Suite 5
Union City, NJ 07087, USA

**Website:** *www. miltonandhugo.com*
**Hotline:** *1- 888-778-0033*
**Email:** *info@miltonandhugo.com*

Ordering Information:
Quantity sales. Special discounts are granted to corporations, associations, and other organizations. For more information on these discounts, please reach out to the publisher using the contact information provided above.

| Library of Congress Control Number: | 2025921259 | |
|---|---|---|
| ISBN-13: | 979-8-89285-618-8 | [Paperback Edition] |
| | 979-8-89285-619-5 | [Hardback Edition] |
| | 979-8-89285-620-1 | [Digital Edition] |

Rev. date: 10/02/2025

# Dedication

To God, without whom I would be nothing.

To my mother, who gave both myself and this book their names. For all that you have done and continue to do for me. For all that you have taught me. My love for you is endless.

To my grandma, for believing in me, for inspiring me, for teaching me the merits of hard work, and for the years of memories I will always cherish.

To my twin, Olivia, for being my other half, for loving me, and for growing up by my side. Thank you for walking beside me on this journey.

To my sister, Lyndsay, for her guidance, love, and sacrifice. For our adventures, our long drives, and everything in between.

To my friends, who listened to me write, rewrite, and cry. Who gave me shoulders to lean on, advice, and support throughout this journey.

To the inspirations for this book plentiful, educational. Thank you for being the reason for the seasons.

there was something unsettling
about bed sheets and
covers
as tangled and confused as the pair in between them
couldn't call them a couple with a shred of accuracy
couldn't call them anything, really
the only solace she felt
the only gratification she received was
watching his chest
slowly rise up
and
fall
down
the only reassurance she had that for a moment
no
for this moment
he was hers
but like the mother bird kicks her
children out to learn to survive
she knew all too well
he would be throwing himself out of the
nest or rather
mess
that he made

sleep is hard to come by nowadays
quiet used to be peaceful
it used to be calm
what once was a silk cocoon of security
is now
making the quiet of the night feel threatening
the antithesis of what it's intended for
ensuring that upon waking the next day
things escape my mouth that shouldn't have
my words are a weapon
of calculated destruction
patience was never my virtue
the exhaustion leaves me questioning
will I ever become more than I am now
more candid, less cruel
vanity is a dish best served insecure

I am tired
not the kind that sleep will cure
though
it probably couldn't hurt
I am the kind of tired that makes your soul weep
the kind of tired that goes deeper than the
black and blue canyons under my eyes
the kind that springs forth tears
from yawning
from yearning for rest
my ability to focus is gone
the kind of tired people only think is possible in fiction
or the movies
the kind of tired that a million and one
distractions
couldn't possibly help
exhausted
with no plan
no cure

sometimes I forget what I look like
when I am fully engaged
fully immersed in what I am doing
living in the moment
for once
rather than hyper focusing on
every
single
detail
but the world will always keep spinning
and reminding you
what you look like
and
who you are

the person who said
absence makes the heart grow fonder
clearly never experienced a firsthand account
absence does no such thing
it allows for the void
in your heart to be
cemented shut
by cynicism
by critical analysis
by empty thrills and
cheap gratification
it teaches hyper independence
in place of healthy codependency
it mirrors insecurities and egos
making it feel like a
puddle
and the ocean
are equidistant

I can't smell stale beer without thinking of you
sitting on the porch
freezing in my less than intelligent choice of clothing
which you seemed to appreciate
so I didn't mind
you put your arm around me
and you laughed
at the way I shook like a nervous animal
I commented on the sky
and you told me about your dad
your life
a white truck
things I really had no interest in
I shared vague snippets of who I was
or rather
who I thought you wanted me to be
you seemed more interested in
physical pursuits and less interested in
my trivial ones

it was a hard realization
whenever I got myself into a predicament
that I realized I never called you
when I needed help
I never called you
when I was in crisis
I never called you
because
I could not depend on you
I depended instead on a man who did not want me
in any other meaningful capacity
other than what he could reap from my figure
his sarcasm matched mine
and the way our spirits seemed to
intertwine
made up for the lack of commitment
made up for the loving insults
and the way he
tempted my fates

I am annoyed by his face
something I have studied
like it was an assignment
like I would be quizzed on
its structure
the angles and curves
that made me fall in love
but I couldn't say that
without scaring him off
so into the subconscious
he went
until one night
admittedly many nights
I dreamt about him
about a little boy of our own
who shares his namesake and my eyes
a crooked smile
the dimple in his right
cheek
and I weep
when I wake up
and I realized it was only a
dream

I have never felt like this before
what a cliche
but it's true
I think of your lips
when I'm kissing another's
trying to distract myself
I think of you all of the time
how you don't think of me
and when you do
it is when you know you cannot have me
my love for you knows no bounds you are the
biggest reason I stay in this godforsaken
town
you make me feel like I am worthy of love
and I hate you for it
we will always share a connection
your words
not mine

you have distorted my vision
in a way I don't think I will ever see clearly again
you care more about me now
that you cannot have me
than you ever did
when I was a potential candidate for your love
I think you heard my heart break when you
said to me
that you could never really see us together
bodies and souls bared
like it was the most casual thing to
roll off of your tongue
when in reality it
stung
hitting my skin like acid
the words cutting my heart with a blade
a dirty cut with a dull blade
I turned away
so you couldn't see the blood pouring
from the wounds you inflicted
and the tears stinging my eyes
because
we didn't do that
we didn't emote in front of one another
you pulled me back to you
to torture me I suppose
when you asked me if I was crying
and I said no
obviously
and you touched my cheeks to check if I was deceiving you
luckily
they were dry
and I whispered
"you are not worth my tears"
I watched your stunned reaction
and you grinned and said to me
that was my best comeback yet

when in reality I
only said it because
I wanted you to always
come back
to
me

lucky number 13
makes me sick
the thought of it
although
I wouldn't care so much about being
number 13
if
I could really be
your number
1

letting go
has to be one of the things I am
most terrible at
even now
sitting here
I could conjure tears from
a million years ago
because
you see
I never learned how to properly grieve
never learned how to
take my heart off of my sleeve and
use that sleeve to
wipe off all shreds of emotion
anything that would make you think I am
human

you are a thousand little vignettes
snippets of pain and love
that encompasses
everything I am
and
everything I want to
become

you say you're waiting to get your life together
you don't want to be
with anyone
until you have your life in order
but the crazy thing about life
and the even crazier thing about love
is it waits for no one
it waits for nothing
you are looking for the next best thing when it is right here
singing your praises
waiving
a flag
to garner your attention
reeking of desperation
looking like the biggest fool for you
reciprocal effort optional here
because that's the funny little thing about love
it hurts so good I can pretend that
you feel the same

day one of no answer
ok he's busy
day two of no answer
ok he's tired
day three of no answer
what did I do wrong
day four no answer
but he's active on socials
day five no answer
it's fine I don't need him
day six no answer
I'm moving on with my life like he was never a part of it
day 7
ding
can I come over?

put your arm down
you said those words to me
in an attempt to pull me closer to you
to your body
a body I have become oh so familiar with
over the course of nearly a year
my nose buried in your chest
my head smashed against you
I gave it my all trying
to stay there
because you looked so peaceful
so content
and I would give every fiber of my being for you to
always look so at ease to always feel so comfortable
however
as anxiety always does rear its ugly head
I felt like I was drowning
physically suffocating
as you were
completely content
and I pulled away
gasping for all the wrong reasons

I didn't delete a single line of
poetry
for this book
until I tried to
write
about
you

coke doesn't mean he loves you
I'm going to the gas station, you need anything?
of course, I said no
I will never admit what I need
the only bubbles I cared about were the
bubby sensations in my stomach that
arose when you looked at me
texted me
used me
hurt me
those lines of white powder gave you a superiority complex
they gave you armor
against a version of yourself you despised
the booger sugar gave you courage
to hate everyone and anyone who reminded you of who you are
and the body you owned before
and as you let yourself in
with a key I provided
and slammed a coke down on my dresser
half drank
you, half baked
I realized
that coke?
doesn't mean he loves you

I don't even want to hurt you anymore
I just want you to go away
I want this limbo to stop
I want this facade to fade
because I don't like her
not one bit
I love you
I am not your friend
I am the catalyst to end the perfection
you think you've created
doing the things I knew you were capable of doing all along
just not for me
because it wasn't that you weren't ready
you weren't waiting for the right time
you were looking for the next best thing
you didn't even need to sell me the lie
I bought it for the price of free
while you used me
at your beck and call
to be relief
I was a clearance coat of arms
discounted and tagged
reliable for warmth and utility
undesirable to the public eye

you are gone now
gone without a trace
so my words were wasted
my time wasted
my love
wasted
but honestly?
what's new
I keep pouring from
an empty vessel
a cup with holes stabbed in every side
hoping that your love would seal them
like your lips sealed over mine
don't worry
I adjusted my expectations and realized
it was better
it was more realistic to discard
the holy vase
then to repair what you broke
repairs are a costly thing, after all

although I physically am usually the
bigger person I hate being it
emotionally
sitting there acting like I don't care
when my throat burns
like you poured acid to try and keep me quiet
then you left
like it was nothing
acting like I would enjoy the fill and the burn
simply because based on my appearance
I must enjoy everything
you tried to shove down my throat
that's the thing about looks
they can be oh so deceiving

hosta's are an invasive species
they also are nearly impossible to eliminate
their roots sunk deep into the earth
and even then,
sometimes,
you think you've pulled the last strands
successfully decimating them from their core
only to see the pale green shoots
and rippled forest hued leaves emerge the next spring I
think that is the type of resilience we should all aspire to
no matter how hard things get
no matter how bad the weather
or the conditions
we may still hold our ground

I think most of us learn our lessons the hard way
because sometimes red flags make us feel special
sometimes a red flag isn't a warning
or a deterrent
sometimes it means
I can change this situation
sometimes leaving the red flag alone means
but I love myself enough not to try

I had never had a sentimental attachment to clothes
in fact
when left to my own devices
I would purchase the same exact t-shirt
in 5 different colors
just to check school clothes shopping off of my list
I would wear anything just to stay covered
fashion was never my forte
when I inevitably outgrew clothing
as a child does
I had no issues
putting it in a white trash bag
sending it out to the donation bin
so why as an adult
do I find it so hard to let go
of the things
and the people
that I outgrow?

delete the number
forgive them
I only healed when I stopped moving backwards

there is a cliche that says something to the effect
of
you can't appreciate the sun without a little rain
the meaning although corny
is true
for it is through the winds in the road
the valleys under the peaks
that I have learned what happiness is again
it can be measured in all sorts of non-quantifiable metrics
in the laughs shared with loved ones
in the smells of a comforting meal
it can be sussed out from the quiet moments too
the moments where I crawl into my mother's bed
to feel that childlike sense of simplicity once again
the moments where I lay awake and reflect back on
how far I have come
and how far yet I have to
go
the realization that I get the privilege of waking up
and paving my own path

and I hope when this is over
not to be described as smart
nor prolific
not even wise
I want to be known for my kindness
for the generosity that seeped from my pores
into the hearts of others
maybe even others who
were not so deserving
I want to be remembered for the way I made people feel
quick wit
and dependable
the friend you call at 2 am when the
lights are a little too bright
and the silence is a little too loud
I want to be reconciled as a person who understood
that my beliefs are not the beliefs of everyone
but that the beliefs I share center on the golden rule
the one that says we should treat others the way
we would want to be treated
maybe we overcompensate
and treat them better than we could ever imagine
treating ourselves
because it is through that treatment of others
through the giving
that we expose our own selfish nature
I hope when all is said and done
the notion that
your happiness is a derivative of my own self worth
should have never been a thing
the perpetual people pleaser grew up
and became more of the same
and I hope when this is over
and the singular grey strands I pull from my hair
outnumber the brunette ones
and the crows feet by my eyes
have lengthened

28

the dark circles under my eyes
have deepend
that I can look backwards and realize
we do the best we know how
that we have always done the best
we knew how

well well well
here we are again
opportunity knocks and you once again
slam the door
or so that's what they believe
I refuse to believe my judgment so poor
I do not accept the idea
the narrative
that my heart is desperate to beat for someone
anyone
but rather
that this is our chance
our moment
to undo the previous hurt I have etched on these pages
so one day we can read this together
and laugh
knowing
it was these words
scribbled down in angst
that kept me
believing in you

there is value in the things that hurt you
there is something about being broken
reduced to the point of tears
gasping for air and help
from this man
a man so broken and tempting
who could easily relinquish both
your way
you need him to throw you
a life preserver in the ocean
when he doesn't even
know how to swim
you need to be rescued but
he can't save you when
he can't even save himself
you plead and beg
giving your body and time
thinking eventually he will see what you have to offer
that's the thing
he knew the whole time
it was his vanity that prevented him
from paradise

I found a man who talks about the future like he isn't afraid
of it
who speaks my name
like it is something sacred
who listens to my thoughts and values
them as if they are his own
who holds me as if it's a privilege to do so
who knows I have potential, but wants to grow with me
I fell for a man who saw my independence
admired it
and then showed me I didn't have to be
always
he
showed me a world where
I could be vulnerable

if you would have told me a year ago
we would have ended up here
I wouldn't have believed you
did it take us hurting one another to bring us together?

let us count all the places I've loved you, shall we?
I've loved you on an app, and in a gas
station in the middle of nowhere
I've loved you as a delivery driver,
sneaking you candy and dinner
at 1 am
I've loved you from a ditch in a town
I never want to return to
I've loved you from a three bedroom house in a college town
from a room that was messy
and complicated
much like the two people in it
you see
I've loved you from a mess that wasn't mine
vacuuming and scrubbing wishing I could wash away
the pain of the months I wasn't allowed to love you
then I loved you from
196 miles away
and eventually from your one-bedroom apartment
with my pillows on your bed
my heart in your hands
I've loved you from a place
where you made five hours of driving seem
effortless
I've loved you from a two-bedroom
apartment in the middle of nowhere
where you still show up because that's
what we do for each other
I've loved you since the day I met you
and I'll continue loving you
always

this too shall pass
for a season cannot sustain forever
they teach us fragility
they show us the beauty of letting go
of having hope
a dangerous thing at times
a change of season can take a heart
once decimated
and piece it together
bit by bit
the change of seasons can show us
that anguish is temporary
joy is fleeting
that
seasons of a broken heart
cannot possibly
last

www.ingramcontent.com/pod-product-compliance
Lightning Source LLC
Chambersburg PA
CBHW022345040426
42449CB00006B/732